România

a photographic memoir | *eine fotografische Erinnerung*

Photos / Fotos:
© Florin Andreescu
Text / Text:
Mariana Pascaru
English translation:
Alistair Ian Blyth
Deutsche Übersetzung:
Lia Gross-Marcu
Grete Klaster-Ungureanu

Editat © AD LIBRI srl
tel/fax: 021-212.35.67, 610.37.92, 210.88.64
e-mail: adlibri@adlibri.ro; www.adlibri.ro
www.florinandreescu.com

Descriere CIP a Bibliotecii Naţionale
FLORIN, ANDREESCU
România: o amintire fotografică – un regard photographique
România: a photographic memoir – eine fotografische Erinnerung
România: un recuerdo fotográfico – un ricordo fotografico
fotografii: Florin Andreescu; text: Mariana Pascaru
trad. fr.: Diane Chesnais; trad. engl.: Alistair Ian Blyth
trad. germ.: Lia Gross-Marcu, Grete Klaster-Ungureanu
trad. sp.: Lucia Mănuş; trad. it.: Ruxandra Tărărescu
Bucureşti: AD LIBRI, 2011
ISBN 978-606-8050-30-0 (versiunea română-franceză)
ISBN 978-606-8050-31-7 (versiunea engleză-germană)
ISBN 978-606-8050-32-4 (versiunea spaniolă-italiană)
913(498)(084)

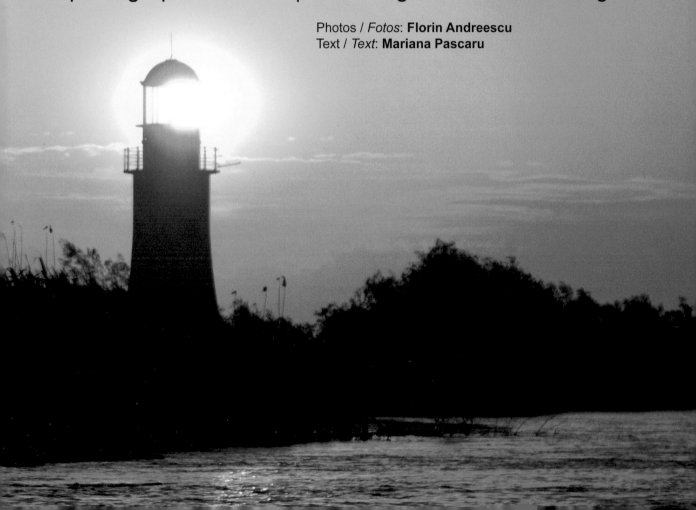

România

a photographic memoir | *eine fotografische Erinnerung*

Photos / *Fotos*: **Florin Andreescu**
Text / *Text*: **Mariana Pascaru**

Romania
a photographic memoir

All places have their own particular way of surprising the traveller. A fulfilling journey sometimes depends on the apparently minor details – on the harmonious rather than the spectacular aspect of a landscape; on the serenity rather than the splendour that envelops one of the world's hidden corners, discovered by chance; on the gentle charm of the provincial settlement rather than the stifling monumentality of the conurbation.

At the core of our memories, we rediscover the tranquillity that enveloped us when we arrived in places just as pure and wild as on the first day of creation, the warmth of locals always ready to tell of legends, the savour of unique traditional recipes, the picturesque ancestral customs. It is from the accumulation of these and other similar impressions that the pure essences of an unforgettable journey are distilled.

This album might be regarded as the "chronicle" of such a journey: it does not attempt to convince you that Romania is the "paradise" of the Balkans, but merely to show you that, to the attentive eye, shards of ineffable beauty reveal themselves here. If you are travelling to Romania for the first time, you will do well to give up any kind of preconception and prepare yourself for surprises, discovering wonders you will never have anticipated.

Romania is that place where the Danubius (or Danube), the sacred river of ancient times, finishes its journey, emptying into the Black Sea after traversing 1,075 kilometres of Romanian territory.

The Roman legions once crossed the Danube on their way to Dacia, the realm of the "immortal" Getes, or Dacians – the ancestors of the modern Romanians – who worshipped Zalmoxis.

After the Romans defeated the Dacians, the south of this territory became a Roman province, named Dacia Felix (in other words, "Fruitful Dacia").

The ethnic mix of Dacians and Romans provided the basis for the emergence of the Romanian people, which has been called "an island of Latinity in a Slavic sea". It is to be wondered just how it was possible for a language of Latin origin, like Italian, Spanish or French, to flourish in a part of Europe that has been reckoned the domain of the Slavic languages par excellence.

Any journey through these regions will reveal to you continually different facets of Romania, almost as if its metamorphoses were inexhaustible. A Romania with the perfume of the Levant; a Romania that preserves the memory of the "little Paris" epoch; a Romania of churches; a sub-Mediterranean Romania, in the vicinity of the Danube; and a Romania of Carpathian mountain peaks are just some of the facets that this astonishing land is waiting to reveal to you.

Today, as Europe transforms itself and searches for a new identity, a journey through Romania yields us significant revelations.

Beyond the hesitations that accompany adoption of the norms for harmonisation imposed by the EU, we shall discover in Romania a land that has always been conscious of its European identity and is endowed with a culture undeniably rooted in European values.

4

Rumänien
eine fotografische Erinnerung

Jeder Ort überrascht den Reisenden in seiner Art. Der Erfolg der Reise hängt manchmal von scheinbar unwichtigen Kleinigkeiten ab – von der Harmonie der Landschaft vielleicht mehr als von ihrer Großartigkeit; von der Heiterkeit und Ruhe, die ein durch Zufall entdeckter verborgener Winkel ausstrahlt, eher als von seinem Glanz; vom lieblichen Zauber der ländlichen Ortschaften und nicht von der erdrückenden Monumentalität der städtischen Ballungszentren. Unser Erinnerungsvermögen lässt uns die Ruhe wiederfinden, die uns umgab, als wir an Stätten weilten, die so unberührt und wildromantisch waren wie am ersten Tag der Schöpfung; die Wärme der Einheimischen, die immer gerne bereit sind, Altüberliefertes zu erzählen; den würzigen Geschmack traditioneller Speisen, einzig in ihrer Art; das Malerische uralter Bräuche. Aus solcherart gesammelten Eindrücken ergeben sich schließlich die bleibenden Erinnerungen an eine unvergessliche Reise.

Dieses Album kann als „Chronik" einer solchen Reise gelten. Es will Sie nicht zu überzeugen versuchen, dass Rumänien das „Paradies" des Balkans sei, es will Ihnen nur zeigen, dass ein aufmerksames Auge hier auf Schritt und Tritt ungeahnte Schönheiten entdecken kann. Falls Sie zum ersten Mal durch Rumänien reisen, ist es angebracht, auf jegliche Vorurteile zu verzichten und sich überraschen zu lassen. So werden Sie Wunderdinge erleben, die Sie gar nicht erwartet haben.

Rumänien ist das Land, wo der uralte heilige Strom Danubius (rumänisch: Dunărea – die Donau) den letzten Teil seines Laufes vollbringt; 1075 km lang durchmisst er es bis zu seiner Mündung ins Schwarze Meer. Die Donau überquerten einst die römischen Truppen auf ihrem Weg nach Dazien, dem Gebiet der „unsterblichen" Geten (oder Dazier) – der Urahnen der Rumänen –, die Zamolxes anbeteten. Nach dem Sieg der Römer über die Dazier wurde der südliche Teil ihres Gebietes zu einer römischen Provinz: Dacia Felix (glückliches Dazien) genannt. Dieses Völkergemisch war die Grundlage, aus der das rumänische Volk hervorging, von dem es heißt, es stelle „eine Oase der Latinität in einem slawischen Meer" dar. In der Tat ist es staunenswert, wie sich eine gleich dem Italienischen, Französischen oder Spanischen aus dem Lateinischen hervorgegangene Sprache in einem Teil Europas hat entwickeln können, der als ausgesprochen slawischer Bereich betrachtet wurde.

Auf jeglicher Reise durch dieses Land werden Sie immer neue Facetten Rumäniens entdecken, als ob seine Metamorphosen unerschöpflich wären. Ein Rumänien von levantinischem Duft, ein Rumänien, das noch an die Zeiten des „kleinen Paris" erinnert, ein Rumänien der Kirchen, ein an der Donau liegendes submediterranes Rumänien, ein Rumänien der Karpatenhöhen. Das sind nur einige wenige Facetten, unter denen sich uns dieses erstaunliche Land darbietet.

Heute, da Europa im Zeichen der Umwandlungen steht und sich auf der Suche nach einer neuen Identität befindet, kann uns eine Reise durch Rumänien zu einigen wichtigen Einsichten verhelfen. Abgesehen von dem Zögern, mit dem die von der EU festgelegten angleichenden Normen angenommen werden, finden Sie hier ein Land vor, das sich seiner Zugehörigkeit zu Europa seit jeher bewusst ist, dessen Kultur den europäischen Werten um nichts nachsteht.

Peaks, stone and water, sun and clouds

If you come Romania, you won't have to worry about any lack of things to do; the hardest thing will be to choose one of the countless tourist itineraries available. Although its surface area does not exceed 240,000 square kilometres, Romania can boast almost every form of geographic relief: mountains, sea, delta, lakes, hills, valleys with winding waterways, caves, ravines, cataracts… The imagination of nature seems to have been inexhaustible in these places.

On the mountain paths that criss-cross the Romanian Carpathians, you will discover landscapes to take your breath away. Invigorated by the pure air of the Romanian high places, you will be overwhelmed by "immense forces", as it is aptly put by the Romanians who flock at weekends to the mountain resorts of the Prahova Valley: Sinaia, the former summer residence of the royal family; Bușteni; Azuga; and Predeal. In summer, the mountains are bathed in the scent of the wildflowers that speckle the meadows or cling to the crags; in winter, they are cloaked in dazzling white, and the excellently equipped ski slopes bustle with activity.

The efforts of those who set out to conquer the Romanian Carpathians always reap rich rewards: every ascent becomes a journey of initiation at the end of which the mountain reveals its mysteries. You can choose between the apparently unassailable Făgăraș range, with its Moldoveanu peak (2544 metres); Piatra Craiului (a crest indented with bluish-white limestone, towering cliff faces, rocky shelfs, crags and scree); the "rocky fortresses" of the Apuseni Mountains (the domain of karst phenomena such as the Ponor Forts, the Living Flame Glacier, the Padiș Plateau, the Galbena, the Warm Someș, and the Râmeți gorges); the Retezat Massif, with its eighty glacial tarns (Bucura, Zănoaga, Tăul Negru, Ana, Lia, Viorica), which is home to a 54,400 hectare national park, declared a Biosphere Reservation; the Maramureș Mountains, traversed by the Vaser Valley, along which runs an old narrow-gauge steam railway; the Gutâi, with its Cockerel Crest, formed of volcanic rocks; the Rodna Mountains, with their numerous glacial features (crests, valleys, moraines); the Rarău Massif, with its bizarre Ladies Rocks; and the volcanically formed Călimani, on whose plateau rise up the twelve Apostles Rocks, which seemingly transport us back to the mythical beginnings of the world.

Nor can we neglect the marvellous hidden face of the mountains of Romania. We refer, of course, to the twelve thousand caves beneath the mountains, whose galleries stretch for more than a thousand kilometres: the Scărișoara Glacier, the Cave of Bears, the Bistrița Cave, the Cave of the Women, the Cave of the Bats, Ialomița Cave, the Cave of Wind, Meziad Cave. The splendours of these "subterranean palaces" seem to have been taken from the world of the Arabian Nights.

The Carpathians have been likened to a "castle of waters", for it is here that hundreds of rivers and streams begin their journey through Romania, representing ninety-eight per cent of the country's network of waters, including the Olt, Mureș, Ialomița, Someș, Argeș, Siret, Jiu, and Râmeț. For the length of the Nera, Turda, Bistrița, Olteț, Runcu (Sohodol), Bicaz, and Tătaru gorges you can witness the millennial, monumental struggle between water and mountain. And these are just a few of the two hundred gorges to be found in Romania.

Romania' s 3,500 lakes each reflect their own unique image of the sky. In the glimmer of their waters are gathered the petrified shadows of the mountains, the restlessly changing clouds and the dazzle of the sun, forming surreal vistas, occasionally disturbed by the glint of airborne wings. In Romania, there are to be found volcanic lakes (St Ana), glacial lakes (Bucura, Zănoaga, Gâlcescu, Bâlea), karst lakes (Iezerul Ighiu), saline lakes (Bottomless Lake, Ursu), natural reservoirs (Roșu), and man-made lakes (the Iron Gates, on the Danube; Izvorul Muntelui or Bicaz, on the Bistrița River; Vidraru, on the Argeș; Vidra, on the Lotru; Scropoasa, on the Ialomița).

1

Gipfel, Fels und Wasser, Sonne und Wolken

Wenn Sie in Rumänien ankommen, brauchen Sie sich keine Sorgen zu machen über die Auswahlmöglichkeiten, die Ihnen zur Verfügung stehen. Schwieriger ist es, sich für eine der zahlreichen touristischen Trassen zu entscheiden, die Ihnen hier vorgeschlagen werden. Obwohl Rumänien nur knappe 240 000 qkm misst, findet man hier so gut wie alle Reliefformen: Gebirge, Meer, Delta, Seen, Berge, Hügel, Flusstäler, Höhlen, Klammen, Engpässe, Wasserfälle…

Entlang der Gebirgspfade, die sich durch die rumänischen Karpaten schlängeln, können Sie atemberaubende Landschaften entdecken. Die herrliche und saubere Gebirgsluft wird Sie trunken machen und „Riesenkräfte" in Ihnen erwecken, wie es die Rumänen behaupten, die am Wochenende die Kurorte des Prahovatales zwischen dem Bucegi-Gebirge und den Baiului-Bergen überfluten: Sinaia, ehemalige Sommerresidenz der königlichen Familie, Bușteni, Azuga, Predeal.

Wer die rumänischen Karpaten erobern will, wird für seine Mühe reichlich belohnt. Jeder Aufstieg ist ein Weg zu neuen Erfahrungen, an dessen Ende einem weitere Geheimnisse des Berges enthüllt werden. Sie können wählen zwischen dem Fogarascher Gebirge (Munții Făgărașului), das schwer zu erobern scheint und dessen höchste Spitze, der Moldoveanu, 2544 m emporragt; dem Königstein (Piatra Craiului) mit seinem gezackten Kamm aus weißgrauem Kalkstein, seinen hohen Wänden, tiefen Schluchten, Felsvorsprüngen und Geröllfeldern; der „steinernen Burg" der Westkarpaten (Munții Apuseni), wo die Karstphänomene zu Hause sind: Cetățile Ponorului, die Eishöhle Focul Viu, das Padiș-Plateau, die Galbenei-Klamm, die Klamm des Warmen Somesch, die Râmeți-Klamm; dem Retezat-Massiv mit seinen 80

Gletscherseen (Bucura, Zănoaga, Tăul Negru, Ana, Lia, Viorica), wo sich auch ein 54 000 Hektar großer Nationalpark befindet, der zum Biosphärenreservat erklärt wurde; den Maramurescher Bergen, vom Wassertal durchzogen, das die alte „Mocănița", eine Schmalspurbahn mit Dampflok, entlangfährt; dem Gutâi-Gebirge mit seinem „Hahnenkamm" (Creasta Cocoșului) aus vulkanischem Gestein; den Rodna-Bergen mit ihren zahlreichen Spuren aus der Eiszeit (Grate, Täler, Kessel, Moränen); dem Rarău-Massiv mit den bizarren Felsgebilden „Pietrele Doamnei".

Auch die erstaunliche, weniger sichtbare Seite der rumänischen Berge können wir nicht unerwähnt lassen; und zwar beziehen wir uns auf die 12 000 Höhlen in ihrem Untergrund, deren Galerien zusammengenommen 1000 km ausmachen: die Eishöhle Scărișoara, die Bärenhöhle, die Bistrița-Höhle, die Weiberhöhle, die Fledermaushöhle, die Ialomița-Höhle, die Windhöhle, die Meziad-Höhle.

Die Karpaten können mit einem „Wasserturm" verglichen werden, denn von hier beginnen Hunderte von Flüssen und Bächen ihren Lauf durch Rumänien, 98% des hydrographischen Netzes des Landes: Olt, Mureș, Ialomița, Someș, Argeș, Siret, Jiu, Râmeți. In den Klammen der Nera, von Turda, der Bistrița, des Olteț, Runcu (Sohodol), Bicaz, Tătaru können Sie die Geschichte der gewaltigen Kämpfe verfolgen, die diese Gewässer Jahrmillionen lang mit dem Berg führen mussten. Und diese Aufzählung umfasst nur einige von den 200 Klammen, die es auf dem Gebiet Rumäniens gibt.

Die rund 3500 Seen, die man in Rumänien finden kann, sind ebenso viele Spiegelbilder des Himmels. Auf ihrer Oberfläche spiegeln sich die starren Schatten der Berge, die unruhig dahinziehenden Wolken, das Glitzern der Sonnenstrahlen – eine surrealistische Landschaft, die ab und zu von darüber hinwegfliegenden Vögeln belebt wird, die sich im Wasser spiegeln. Es gibt hier Seen vulkanischen Ursprungs (der Sankt-Anna-See), Gletscherseen (Bucura, Zănoaga, Gâlcescu, Bâlea), Karstseen (Iezerul Ighiu), Salzseen (Lacul fără fund, Ursu), natürliche Stauseen (Lacul Roșu), antropische Seen (Porțile der Fier – das Eiserne Tor – an der Donau, Izvorul Muntelui oder Bicaz an der Bistrița, Vidraru am Argeș, Vidra am Lotru, Scropoasa an der Ialomița).

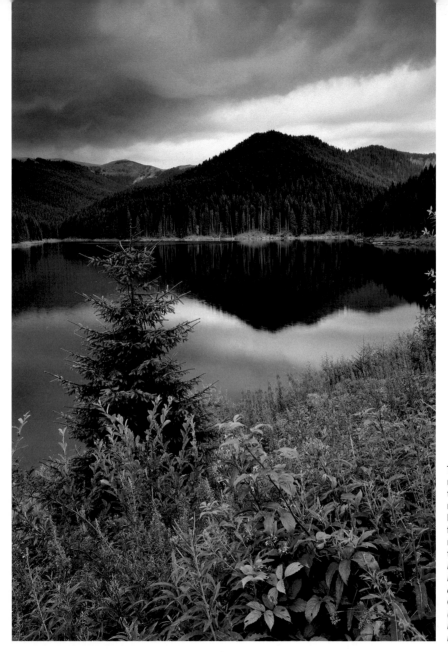

The Bolboci natural
reservoir, formed by
the River Ialomiţa in the
middle of the Bucegi, and
Lacul Roşu, formed at the
foot of the Hăşmaşu Mare
mountain by the barrier of
the Bicaz Valley
*Die natürlichen Stauseen
Bolboci, am Flusslauf
der Ialomiţa im Bucegi-
Gebirge, und Lacu Roşu
(der Rote See), am Fuße des
Hăşmaşu-Mare-Gebirges,
nahe der Bicaz-Klamm*

The Buceș-Vulcan Pass (725 m), traversed by the road linking Abrud and Brad
Der Buceș-Vulcan-Pass (725 m), über den die Nationalstraße von Brad nach Abrud verläuft

The Scărița-Belioara Reserve in the Muntele Mare Massiv, Apuseni Mountains
Das Naturschutzgebiet Scărița-Belioara, auf dem Muntele-Mare-Massiv, in den Westkarpaten

The high altitude Transfăgărăşan highway, with a length
of ninety kilometres, traverses the Făgăraş Mountains,
reaching the shores of the Bâlea Lake (2034 m).
Die Transfogarascher, eine 90 km lange Höhenstraße, die
das Fogarascher Gebirge überquert und auch am Rande des
2034 m hoch gelegenen Gletschersees Bâlea vorbeiführt.

The Râmeț Gorges, view from Ponor village (previous pages)
Die Râmețului-Klamm, vom Dorf Ponor aus gesehen (vorherige Seiten)

The scattered homesteads of Șirnea village, Rucăr-Bran corridor
Verstreute Bauernhöfe des Dorfes Șirnea, im Rucăr-Bran-Pass
Rimetea village, Alba county, at the foot of Secuilor Summit
Das Dorf Rimetea im Kreis Alba, am Fuße des Gipfels Piatra Secuiului

Fundata village, with the Bucegi Mountains in the background
Das Dorf Fundata, mit dem Bucegi-Gebirge im Hintergrund

The Bukowina region, winter
Winter in der Bukowina

The Glacier Caves at Scărişoara and the Living Flame Glacier in the Apuseni Mountains
Die Eishöhlen Scărişoara und Focul Viu in den Westkarpaten (Munţii Apuseni)

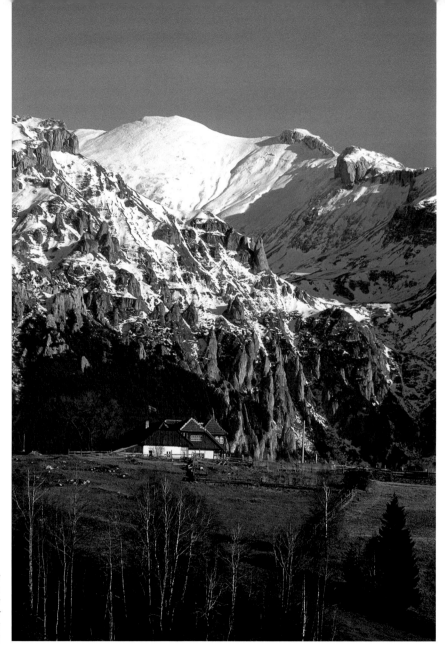

Houses scattered over
the hills of the Rucăr-Bran
Corridor
*Vereinzelt stehende Häuser
auf den Höhen längs des
Rucăr-Bran-Durchbruchs*

First snows in Cavnic, Maramureş
Der erste Schnee in Cavnic, Maramureş

Beuşniţa Waterfall, Caraş-Severin
Der Beuşniţa-Wasserfall, Caraş-Severin

Jina village, Mărginimea Sibiului (previous pages)
Das Dorf Jina, Mărginimea Sibiului (vorherige Seiten)

Măguri-Răcătău village, Cluj county. Alma Vii settlement, consisting
of a fortified church from the sixteenth century
*Das Dorf Măguri-Răcătău, Kreis Cluj. Das Dorf Alma Vii (Almen), mit
Kirchenburg aus dem XVI. Jahrhundert*

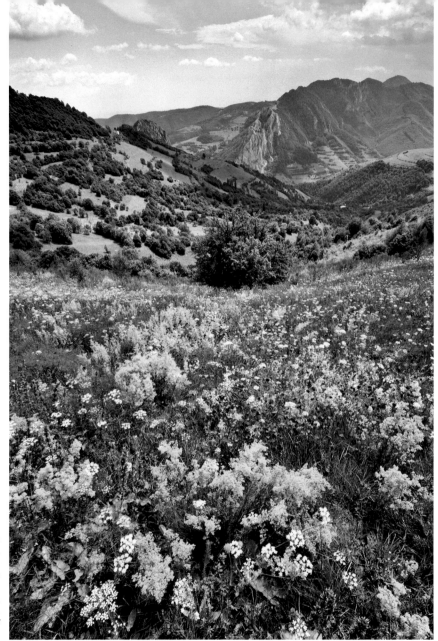

The Coştilei slope in the
Bucegi Mountains
*Der Coştilei-Steilhang im
Bucegi-Gebirge*

View towards
the Râmeţ Gorges
*Aussicht auf
die Râmeţului-Klamm*

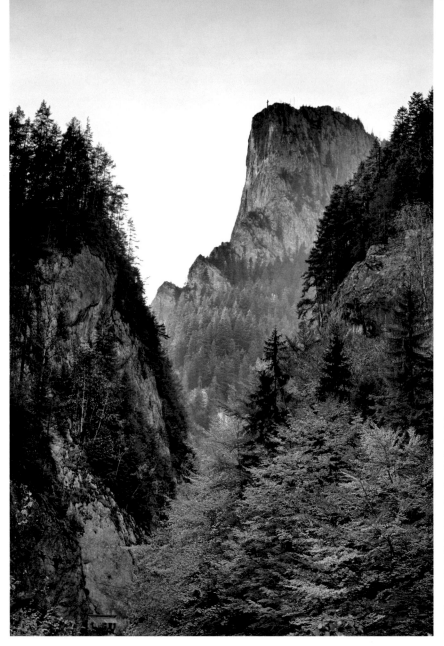

Altarului Crag (1,154 m)
in the Bicaz Gorges
*Piatra Altarului (der
Altarstein, 1.154 m) in der
Bicaz-Klamm*

The Poiana Ruscă
Mountains, the heart
of Pădureni Country,
between the Cerna and
Mureş valleys
*Das Poiana-Ruscă-
Gebirge, im Herzen
des als „Ţinutul
Pădurenilor" („Gegend der
Waldarbeiter") bekannten
Gebietes, zwischen den
Flusstälern der Cerna und
des Mureş gelegen*

The peasant fortress of Râşnov, built in the thirteenth century
Die Bauernburg in Râşnov (Rosenau), im XIII. Jahrhundert errichtet

The sanctuary at Sarmizegetusa Regia (Hunedoara county)
Das Heiligtum von Sarmizegetusa Regia (Kreis Hunedoara)

Rhododendrons, common in the high Carpathians, can also be found in the Bucegi Mountains, on Furnica Summit.
Die Siebenbürgische Alpenrose (Rhododendron kotschyi) ist überall in den rumänischen Karpaten anzutreffen, so auch auf dem Furnica-Gipfel im Bucegi-Gebirge.

The geological and geomorphic reserve of Râpa Roşie, on the right slope of the Sebeş Valley
Das geologische und geomorphologische Reservat Râpa Roşie (Rote Schlucht) am rechten Ufer des Sebeş-Flusses

2

An expanse of waters and land

Many are the revelations of the murmuring Danube on its Romanian stretch: a spectacular gorge, 144 kilometres in length, along which can be found the majestic Cauldrons; banks along which has sprouted sub-Mediterranean vegetation (even though we are in a zone under continental climactic influence!); mysterious forms of karst relief; a delta which can truly named a paradise for plants and animals of all kinds; and the numerous vestiges of history…

There is a spirit of history that hovers over these vestiges, not allowing them to conceal their mysteries for all time. We should not forget the flourishing Greek colonies of the Black Sea coast, founded in the seventh and sixth centuries B.C.: Histria, Callatis (Mangalia), and Tomis (Constanţa), the latter of which was sung in the *Tristia* and *Epistulae ex Ponto* of the Latin poet Ovid, exiled here by the Emperor Augustus in the first century A.D. Nor should we forget how the Roman legions crossed the Danube on their way to Dacia. The foot of the bridge built by Apollodoros of Damascus in 103-105 A.D. at the orders of the Emperor Trajan can still be found at Drobeta-Turnu Severin. Other vestiges from Roman times include the Herculanean Baths, ruined forts, and ancient roads, such as that built along the Danube, as attested by the *Tabula Traiana*, carved into the rock at the point where the Danube emerges from the Cauldrons. In the locality of Adamclisi, in the Dobrogea region, the ruins of the *Tropaeum Traiani* and the triumphal monument erected in honour of the Emperor Trajan's victory over the Dacians evoke the shadows of the past before our very eyes.

A journey down the Danube would not be complete without short stops at its wonderful ports: Orşova, Drobeta-Turnu Severin, Calafat, Turnu Măgurele, Giurgiu, Călaraşi, Cernavodă, Brăila, Galaţi, Tulcea, Sulina.

The head of Decebal, sculpted between 1994 and 2004 from a huge crag in the Danube gorges, near Orşova and the Iron Gates
Der Kopf des Daker-Königs Decebalus, eine riesige Felsskulptur am Ufer der Donau, in der Nähe von Orşova (Orschowa) und Porţile de Fier (Eisernes Tor), zwischen 1994 und 2004 geschaffen

Babacai – an enigmatic rock rises from the waters of the Danube (following page)
Babacai – ein mysteriöser Felsblock mitten in der Donau (nächste Seite)

Wasser und Erde so weit das Auge reicht

Auf dem Gebiet Rumäniens bietet die murmelnd dahinfließende Donau so manche Offenbarung: einen beeindruckenden Engpass in einer Gesamtlänge von 144 km, innerhalb dessen der majestätische Sektor der „Kessel" (Cazane) besonders auffällt; ferner die mediterrane Vegetation an den Ufern (obwohl wir uns in einem Gebiet befinden, das unter dem Einfluss des kontinentalen Klimas steht); interessante Karstformationen fallen ins Auge, und schließlich folgt das Donaudelta, das man zu Recht ein „Paradies" der Pflanzen und Tiere aller Art nennen kann und wo die Spuren der Vergangenheit zahllos sind.

Es herrscht hier ein Geist der Geschichte, der über den Zeugnissen alter Zeiten schwebt und nicht zulässt, dass diese in Vergessenheit geraten. Es wäre unverzeihlich zu vergessen, dass es einst am Ufer des Schwarzen Meeres blühende griechische Kolonien gegeben hat, die im 7.-6. Jahrhundert v.Chr. gegründet wurden: Histria, Callatis (Mangalia), Tomis (Constanța). Es wäre unverzeihlich zu vergessen, dass die römischen Truppen über die Donau setzten und ins Herz Daziens vordrangen. Ein Pfeiler der Brücke, die auf Befehl des Kaisers Trajan vom Architekten Apollodor von Damaskus in den Jahren 103-105 n.Chr. gebaut wurde, hat sich bei Drobeta-Turnu Severin bis heute erhalten. Andere Spuren aus jener Zeit finden wir in Herkulesbad (Băile Herculane) – die Thermen –, ferner Ruinen römischer Kastren, Spuren antiker Straßen, darunter die entlang der Donau, wie es die Inschrift der Tabula Traiana besagt, die auf Befehl des Kaisers da in den Fels geschlagen wurde, wo die Donau die „Kleinen Kessel" verlässt. In der Gemeinde Adamclisi, in der Dobrudscha, sind es die Ruinen einer römischen Festung und das Tropaeum Traiani, das zu Ehren des Sieges Kaiser Trajans über die Dazier errichtete Triumphdenkmal, welche die Schatten der Vergangenheit wecken und uns vor Augen führen.

Eine Reise entlang der Donau wäre nicht komplett, würde man nicht auch in den schönen Hafenstädten Orșova, Drobeta-Turnu Severin, Calafat, Giurgiu, Călărași, Cernavodă, Brăila, Galați, Tulcea, Sulina kurz verweilen.

A snapshot from the world of crested pelicans, a protected species
Schnappschuss aus der Vogelwelt der Krauskopfpelikane – eine unter Naturschutz stehende Art

Delta fisherman (following page)
Fischer im Donaudelta (nächste Seite)

In the Danube Delta, the largest wetland reserve in Europe (2,681 square kilometres), we find expanses of water and land teeming with primordial, luxuriant vegetation. We lose ourselves in groves of white willows or in mixed woods of poplar, oak, ash, elm, wild apple and pear. This is the domain of creeping plants, such as lianas and wild vines, which burgeon everywhere. The vast expanses of rushes and bulrushes create an unforgettable decor.

The waters stretch into the distance covered in wonderful carpets of white and yellow lily-pads, here and there broken by islands of floating vegetation. Everything here teems with life: the air hums to the flight of birds (pelicans, swans, egrets, white-tailed eagles); beneath the waters dart fishes (sturgeon, sterlet, perch, pike, carp, crucian).

This exotic delta, between the river arms of the Chilia, Sulina and Sfântu Gheorghe, in which have been identified more than 1,200 species of plants and trees, 300 species of bird, and 100 species of fish, has been declared a UNESCO Biosphere Reserve.

Common tern –*Sterna hirundo*
Flussseeschwalben – Sterna hirundo

Avocet – *Recurvirostra avosetta*
Säbelschnäbler – Recurvirostra avosetta

Im Donaudelta, dem größten Feuchtgebiet-Reservat Europas (2681 qkm), finden wir riesige Wasserflächen und Land, auf dem es üppig grünt und blüht, wild wie am ersten Tag. Wir verirren uns in Auenwäldern von Weißweide oder aber in Mischwäldern, in denen Schwarzpappeln, Espen, Eichen, Eschen, Ulmen, Wildäpfel- und -birnbäume wachsen. Schlingpflanzen wie Lianen und wilder Wein wuchern und vernetzen alles. Riesige Flächen, mit Schilf, Rohr, Riedgras und Binsen bewachsen, bilden ein Dekor, das man so leicht nicht vergessen kann. So weit das Auge reicht, sind die Wasserflächen mit herrlichen Teppichen von weißen und gelben Seerosen bedeckt, ab und zu von schwimmenden Schilfinseln unterbrochen. Alles ist hier voller Leben: die Luft vibriert vom Flügelschlag der Vögel, die von überall auftauchen (Pelikane, Schwäne, Brandgänse, Reiher,

Löffler, Blässhühner, Seeadler); unter der Wasseroberfläche sieht man die Fische herumschwimmen (Hausen, Stör, Sternhausen, Sterlet, Barsch, Hecht, Karpfen, Karausche). Dieses so exotische Delta, das zwischen den Flussarmen Chilia, Sulina und Sfântu Gheorghe liegt und in dem mehr als 1200 Pflanzen- und Baumarten, 300 Vogelarten, 100 Fischarten identifiziert wurden, ist seitens der UNESCO zu einem Biosphärenreservat erklärt worden.

Spoonbills in the Danube Delta
Biosphere Reserve
Löffler im Biosphärenreservat
Donaudelta

Colony of cormorants
Kormorankolonie

Bird of prey on the hunt
The great crested grebe – *Podiceps cristatus*
Whooper swan – *Cygnus cygnus*
Squacco heron – *Ardeola ralloides*

Raubvögel auf der Suche nach Beute
Der Haubentaucher – Podiceps cristatus
Singschwäne – Cygnus cygnus
Rallenreiher – Ardeola ralloides

Romania has the rare privilege of having an opening onto the Black Sea, of approximately two hundred and forty kilometres. Along the southern Romanian coast, which stretches from the Midia Cape to Vama Veche, we can encounter both wild rocky shores and exotic beaches of fine sand. The hypnotically purling waves of the "Tranquil Sea" (the Pontus Euxinus, as it was known in antiquity) and the sunrises seen from its shores are an overwhelming, unforgettable experience.

In summer, the resorts of Mamaia, Năvodari, Eforie Nord, Eforie Sud, Olimp, Costinești, Neptun, Jupiter, Venus, Saturn and Mangalia teem with thousands of tourists here to enjoy the sun and beaches. Constanța, built on the ruins of a Greek colony (Tomis) from the seventh century B.C., owes its remarkable development to King Carol I, during whose reign the maritime port was modernised, by engineer Anghel Saligny. In this period, numerous hotels were also built, as well as the impressive Casino.

Rumänien erfreut sich des seltenen Vorteils, eine etwa 240 km lange Küste entlang des Schwarzen Meeres zu besitzen. In ihrem südlichen Teil, der vom Kap Midia bis Vama Veche reicht, trifft man sowohl auf wilde Felsküsten als auch auf exotische Strände mit feinstem Sand. Das hypnotische Rauschen der Wellen dieses „freundlichen Meeres" (Pontus Euxinus, wie es in der Antike genannt wurde), die Sonnenaufgänge, die man vom Ufer aus betrachten kann, sind geradezu berauschende Schauspiele, wie man sie so bald nicht vergisst. Wer sich weit aufs Meer hinauswagt, könnte mit ein wenig Glück die Spiele der freundlichen Delphine beobachten, die in diesem Meer leben. Die Seebäder Mamaia, Năvodari, Eforie Nord, Eforie Sud, Olimp, Costineşti, Neptun, Jupiter, Venus, Saturn, Mangalia sind im Sommer von Tausenden Touristen bevölkert, die hierher kommen, um sich an der Sonne und dem Meereswasser zu erfreuen. Constanţa, auf den Ruinen einer griechischen Kolonie aus dem 7. Jahrhundert v.Chr. erbaut, verdankt seinen bemerkenswerten Aufstieg König Carol I., während dessen Regierungszeit man den Seehafen modernisierte, eine Arbeit, die unter Leitung des Ingenieurs Anghel Saligny durchgeführt wurde. Zur selben Zeit entstanden auch zahlreiche Hotels und das schmucke Kasino.

Rapeseed fields stretching as far as the horizon and wild peonies are typical of the landscape of Dobrudja near Babadag.
Rapsfelder bis hin zum Horizont und wilde Pfingstrosen prägen die Landschaft der Dobrudscha in der Umgebung von Babadag.

The Danube carries us onwards, deeper into Romania…
Und die Donau trägt uns weiter, anderen Zielen in Rumänien entgegen...

Strip of sub-tropical forest among the Letea sand dunes, Danube Delta
Subtropische Waldstreifen zwischen den Sanddünen in Letea, Donaudelta

At the edge of the plains of Dobrudja wind turbines have
begun to make their appearance.
*In der Dobrudscha sind immer mehr Windräder am Rande
der Felder zu sehen.*

3

Villages, people, traditions and faith

You have not seen Romania until you visit its villages, with their picturesque, archaic atmosphere, which is paradoxically not at all anachronistic, given that everything throbs with life. You will be able to feast your ears on the ballads, doinas (traditional songs) and carols, and your eyes on the colourful peasant rugs, which are woven on the loom at home and used as carpets or to decorate the walls. Only then will you be able to understand the depths of the folk spirit. You would also do well to visit the potters' workshops at Horezu (Vâlcea County), Marginea and Rădăuți (Suceava County), Vama (Satu Mare County), which religiously preserve the secrets of ancient techniques for making ceramic vases, decorated with folk motifs of exquisite taste. Then you should observe the amazing metamorphoses of wood: in Bukowina, Maramureş or the Apuseni Mountains, there flourishes a veritable culture of woodworking, and the meticulously carved porches of churches and houses are like jewels.

The traditions and customs of the Romanians have a rarely encountered savour. The people hereabouts are closely attached to their customs. At a time when city folk are homogenising everything and forgetting the essence of the things amongst which they dwell, the Romanian peasant refuses to give up his beliefs and stubbornly preserves the last remnants of his ancestral pastoral culture. In the mountains and hills of certain areas of Romania – especially the Sibiu area

and the Rucăr-Bran corridor – you may still meet shepherds who know the ancient methods of making cheese, cottage cheese and "bulz" (a dish of cheese and polenta). Every year, there are dozens of festivals all over Romania which revive rituals whose real meanings have been partially forgotten but which nevertheless still preserve the essential. For example, the Maidens' Market at Muntele Găina, an ancient pastoral festival, has already won over all Romanians. Every year, on the Sunday before Saint Elijah's Day (20 July), thousands of people from all over the country repeat the sacred ritual of making the ascent to the glade situated at the top of the mountain, at a height of 1,467 metres. Each spring, in Hoteni, Maramureş, the Tânja on Mara Mountain is held, a rural festival centred on the most industrious householder in the village: the first to go out to plough that year (previous pages).

It is not possible to speak of the Romanian Christmas and New Year festivities without mentioning the alluring aroma of "cozonac" (a traditional cake), the carols, the rituals connected to the cutting of the pig, and the shouts of the bands of masked revellers, dressed as bears, who roam the villages wishing householders a plentiful year. At Easter, Romanians prepare "pasca" (a kind of cheesecake) and masterfully decorate eggs: each one of these eggs, painstakingly painted with dozens of traditional motifs, in the predominant colours of red, yellow and black, may be regarded as a miniature work of art.

In the villages still persists the belief in a "magical world" dominated by supernatural forces, inhabited by demons, pixies, fairies, ghosts and witches. Romanian superstitions recreate an archaic universe, in which each element is redolent with meaning. Peasants still know how to weave wonderful tales, and everyday talk is still coloured by countless wise sayings reminiscent of the sagacity of the Orient.

The world beyond is a living presence for these peasants. They know how to honour their dead, with certain festivals being exclusively dedicated to the remembrance of departed souls. On the Day of the Dead, which is celebrated each autumn, thousands of candles are lit by the faithful and gleam in the cemeteries until the dawn of the next day.

3

Dörfer, Menschen,
Traditionen und Glauben

Falls Sie Rumänien besucht und nicht auch in den Dörfern mit ihrer malerischen archaischen Atmosphäre geweilt haben, die gar nicht anachronisch wirkt, da hier überall das Leben pulsiert, haben Sie noch nicht alles gesehen. Falls Sie Rumänien besucht und nicht auch einen gemütlichen Plausch mit seinen Menschen geführt haben, für welche das Wahren der Traditionen selbstverständlich ist, haben Sie den Zauber des Landes noch nicht entdeckt. Erfreuen Sie Ihr Herz mit Doinen (traditionelle schwermütige Volkslieder), alten Balladen und althergebrachten Weihnachtsliedern und Ihre Augen an den bunten Wandbehängen und Teppichen, die von den Bäuerinnen noch selbst am Webstuhl gefertigt werden. Erst dann werden Sie den Kunstsinn und die Lebensweise dieses Volkes erahnen. Besuchen Sie unbedingt die Werkstätten der Töpfer in Horezu (Kreis Vâlcea), in Marginea und Rădăuţi (Kreis Suceava), in Vama (Kreis Satu Mare), die die Geheimnisse der uralten Techniken zur Herstellung der Keramikgefäße heilig halten. Das Dekor dieser Volkskeramik ist immer von vollendetem Geschmack. Auch die erstaunliche Metamorphose des Holzes müssen Sie verfolgen. In der Maramureş, der Bukowina oder in den Westkarpaten, wo geradezu eine Zivilisation des Holzes aufgeblüht ist, gleichen die Häuser mit ihren offenen Veranden und die wunderbar verzierten Holzkirchen wahren Schmuckstücken.

Die Traditionen und Sitten der Rumänen haben etwas ganz Besonderes an sich. Die Menschen halten große Stücke auf ihre Bräuche. Im Berg- und Hügelland gewisser Gebiete in Rumänien – vor allem in der Gegend von Hermannstadt (Sibiu) oder im Durchbruch Rucăr-Bran – kann man immer wieder die Schafherden mit ihren Hirten antreffen, welche die alten Techniken der Milchverarbeitung zu Käse und „urda" (Molkekäse) und die Zubereitung des „bulz" (mit Käse gefüllte Maisbreiklöße) noch bestens kennen. Jahr für Jahr werden in allen Regionen Rumäniens an zahlreichen Feiertagen Rituale wieder belebt, deren wahrer Sinn zum Teil schon verloren ging, doch der festliche Geist blieb erhalten. Alle diese Bräuche stehen mit dem Leben der Hirten, mit ihrer Tätigkeit im Laufe des Jahres in enger Verbindung. Jedes Jahr wird in Hoteni, in der Maramureş, das Frühlingsfest „Tânjaua de pe Mara" („Die Pflugdeichsel von der Mara") veranstaltet, in dessen Mittelpunkt der fleißigste Landwirt des Dorfes – der als Erster seinen Acker gepflügt hat – steht (Foto - vorherige Seiten).

Von den rumänischen Festlichkeiten anlässlich der Weihnachtsfeiertage und des Neujahrs können wir nicht sprechen, ohne den verlockenden Duft des Backwerks zu erwähnen, die Lieder und Zurufe der Maskierten (Bären, Ziegen, Pferdchen), die durch die Dörfer ziehen und den Hauswirten ein gesegnetes Jahr wünschen; auch die Rituale im Zusammenhang mit dem Schweineschlachten und der Verarbeitung des Fleisches sind erwähnenswert. Zu Ostern backen die rumänischen Frauen einen speziellen Osterkuchen, „pască" genannt, und verzieren die Eier mit viel Geschick. Jedes einzelne dieser peinlich genau dekorierten Eier weist Dutzende von traditionellen Mustern und ein paar vorherrschende Farben (rot, gelb, schwarz) auf und könnte ein kleines Kunstwerk genannt werden.

In den Dörfern glaubt man noch an die „magische Welt", die von überirdischen Kräften gelenkt und von Dämonen, Elfen, Feen, Gespenstern und Zauberinnen bevölkert wird. Der Aberglaube der Rumänen lässt eine archaische Weltanschauung erkennen, in der jedes Element seine Bedeutung hat. Die Bauern verstehen es meisterhaft, Schwänke zu erzählen, ihre Sprache ist immer bilderreich, und die vielen geistreichen Aussprüche, die ihre Alltagssprache würzen, erinnern irgendwie an die Weisheiten des Orients.

The blessing of the victuals at Easter
Segnung der traditionellen Osterspeisen

The unaffected way in which children wear traditional costume is a striking feature of Romania.
Ein weiterer erstaunlicher Anblick in Rumänien: die Selbstverständlichkeit, mit der die Kinder Tracht und Bräuche der Eltern übernehmen.

The everyday life of young people in Romania does not seem much different from that of their western counterparts. They have the same musical tastes, they wear the same fashions, and they are up to date with all the latest technology. On festive days, however, they rediscover the picturesque beauty of their ancestral traditions.

Im alltäglichen Leben scheinen sich die jungen Leute aus Rumänien nicht von denen des Westens zu unterscheiden. Sie bevorzugen die gleiche Musik, kleiden sich nach neuester Mode, kennen die neuesten Entdeckungen auf dem Gebiet der Technik. An Feiertagen jedoch entdecken sie wieder die malerische Schönheit der Bräuche ihrer Ahnen.

Moieciu village, against the backdrop of the Bucegi Mountains (following pages)
Das Dorf Moieciu, mit dem Bucegi-Gebirge im Hintergrund (nächste Seiten)

The life of the Romanians seems always to have been dominated by a profound sense of the religious. It might be said that Romania, which is pre-eminently Orthodox, is a land of churches, hermitages and monasteries. The life of the people in each settlement in these regions centres around a church, which is regarded as the *axis mundi*. Sheltered from the stress and bustle of our everyday life, the hermitages and monasteries of Romania, whence have withdrawn monks in search of *hesykhia* (or spiritual tranquillity), leading lives of prayer and fasting, are wonderful places in which to reflect and to rediscover God.

Das Leben der Rumänen war anscheinend seit je her von einem tief religiösen Gefühl durchdrungen. Man kann sagen, dass Rumänien – ein vorwiegend orthodoxes Gebiet – ein Land der Kirchen, Einsiedeleien und Klöster ist. Das Leben der Menschen einer jeden Niederlassung in diesem Land ist auf die Kirche ausgerichtet, sie ist der Mittelpunkt ihres Lebens. Die Einsiedeleien und Klöster liegen abseits des Lärms und der Hetze unseres heutigen Alltags. Hier, wohin sich die Mönche zurückzogen, um fern der profanen Welt in Einsamkeit ein Leben mit Fasten und Beten zu führen, gibt es herrliche Orte, wo man in sich gehen und Gott wieder finden kann.

The rupestrian church of Şinca Veche, Braşov county, and the Grotto of Dionysius the Spinner, Buzău county
Die Höhlenkirche von Şinca Veche, Kreis Braşov, und die Grotte des Dionisie Torcătorul, Kreis Buzău

The historical Romanian province of Moldavia is celebrated throughout the world for its splendid churches and monasteries, founded by god-fearing Moldavian boyars (Voroneț, Putna, Humor, Sucevița, Moldovița, Arbore, Bogdana, Pătrăuți, Bălinești, Probota, Dragomirna). The beauty of the frescoes, painted in inimitable hues of blue, red, yellow and green, which adorn the exterior walls of some monasteries, is overwhelming; these ancient images, which recount the sacred and profane history of the world, are unforgettable.

Die historische rumänische Provinz Moldau ist in aller Welt wegen ihrer wunderbaren Kirchen und Klöster berühmt, die von gottesfürchtigen moldauischen Herrschern und Bojaren gestiftet wurden (Voroneț, Putna, Humor, Sucevița, Moldovița, Arbore, Bogdana, Pătrăuți, Probota, Dragomirna). Die Schönheit der Fresken, die in unverwechselbaren blauen, roten, gelben und grünen Farbtönen ausgeführt sind und die Außenwände einiger Klosterkirchen bedecken, ist geradezu überwältigend. Nachdem man diese alten Bilder gesehen hat, die die heilige und profane Geschichte der Welt wieder aufleben lassen, ist es unmöglich, sie jemals wieder zu vergessen.

The exterior frescoes of Voroneț Monastery, founded by Stephen the Great in 1488, and the vault of the church of Moldovița Monastery, founded in 1532 by Petru Rareș
Außenwandmalereien der Klosterkirche Voroneț (1488), eine Stiftung des Fürsten Stefan des Großen, und Gewölbe der Klosterkirche Moldovița (1532), eine Stiftung des Fürsten Petru Rareș

Compared with the massive stone churches, small wooden churches provide a different order of spatiality. Nowhere is it more fitting than in Maramureș to experience the full splendour achieved by the art of woodworking in Romania. Impressive examples of peasant art and expressions of rural spirituality, the wooden churches of Maramureș, with their tapering spires reaching to the heavens, seem to have overcome the essentially perishable nature of the material from which they were fashioned.

Im Vergleich zu den massiven Kirchen aus Stein ist der Innenraum der kleinen Holzkirchen anders eingeteilt. Um den hohen Grad zu veranschaulichen, den die Kunst der Holzbauten in Rumänien erreicht hat, ist die Maramureș wohl der geeignetste Ort. Die Holzkirchen von hier, mit ihren schlanken Türmen, die gleichsam den Himmel zu erreichen suchen, sind bewundernswerte Beispiele der bäuerlichen Kunst, ein Ausdruck der dörflichen Spiritualität. Man hat den Eindruck, dass sie die Vergänglichkeit des Elements, aus dem sie gebaut wurden, überwunden haben.

The Church on the Hill, Ieud, and the church of Botiza
Die Kirche „auf dem Berg" in Ieud und die Kirche in Botiza

What immediately attracts our attention when we travel through Romania is the large number of churches, to be found at every step. Most of them are over a hundred years old. We naturally wonder as to what it might mean. Why did the people of these parts feel the need to build so many places of worship, these veritable architectural wonders, so beautifully decorated and richly endowed? The old folk will answer simply: so that God might help them in all their affairs.

Was uns bei einer Reise durch Rumänien besonders auffällt, ist die große Anzahl von Gotteshäusern, die man so gut wie überall antrifft. Die meisten sind Hunderte Jahre alt. Was hat das zu bedeuten? fragen wir uns zu Recht. Warum haben die hier lebenden Menschen das Bedürfnis empfunden, so viele Sakralbauten zu errichten, wahre architektonische Wunderwerke, schön ausgeschmückt und mit Schenkungen reich bedacht? Die hier ansässigen Alten hätten gleich eine einfache Antwort parat: „Damit Gott ihnen in allem hilft, was sie sich vornehmen."

Sinaia Monastery, built in the late seventeenth century, the Corbii de Piatră rupestrian church, which preserves some of the oldest murals in Wallachia, and the fortress-like Govora Monastery, founded in the heart of Oltenia in the fifteenth century.

Kloster Sinaia, Ende des XVII. Jh. erbaut, die Höhlenkirche in Corbii de Piatră, die einige der ältesten Malereien der Walachei bewahrt, und Kloster Govora, im XV. Jh. ähnlich einer Festung im Herzen Olteniens erbaut.

At the centre of the rural settlements founded by Saxon colonists in the Romanian province of Transylvania in the twelfth century there stand fortified churches, which once served as places of refuge in times of danger. Many of these fortress-like stronghold churches, built mainly after the Tartar invasion of 1241, have been preserved.

Im Zentrum der alten Dörfer, die von den deutschen Kolonisten – den Siebenbürger Sachsen – in der rumänischen Provinz Transsilvanien im 12. Jahrhundert gegründet wurden, steht die Kirchenburg, die im Falle einer Gefahr auch als Zufluchtsort diente. Heute noch stehen viele dieser Wehrkirchen, die wie kleine Burgen aussehen; die meisten von ihnen entstanden nach dem Tatareneinfall im Jahr 1241.

The fortified churches of Prejmer,
Dealu Frumos, Cincu and Viscri
Die Wehrkirchen in Prejmer (Tartlau), Dealu Frumos (Schönberg), Cincu (Großschenk) und Viscri (Deutschweißkirch)

Romania: images from a world
of religious faith
*Rumänien – Bilder aus einer
Welt des Glaubens*

Cityscapes

The blend of old and new that can be met in Romanian towns is sometimes disconcerting. Constructions of concrete and steel and streets full of the dizzying din so characteristic of our times are to be found alongside piazzas flanked by magnificent edifices in the Baroque, Renaissance, Secession or Neo-classical styles, as well as quiet streets shaded by chestnut trees… Here and there can be discovered the scars left by the communist regime, beneath whose nefarious rule Romania endured for almost half a century. Thousands of old houses were demolished in Romanian towns during that period, to make way for homogenous, ugly apartment blocks. Since the Revolution of 1989, which led to the overthrow of dictator Nicolae Ceaușescu and the istallation of democracy, a market economy has been established. Since then, building work has gone on at fever pitch seemingly everywhere, resulting in a spectacular and rapid transformation in the appearance of the old cities. The urban trend now represents a shift away from the centre and a valorisation of the outskirts.

Bucharest, the capital of Romania, is a genuine European city, with magnificent buildings: the National Savings Bank, the National Museum of History, the Military Club, the National Museum of Art (formerly the Royal Palace), the Central University Library (formerly the Palace of the Carol I University Foundation), the Romanian Athenaeum, the George Enescu Museum (the Cantacuzino Palace), the Municipality of Bucharest Museum of History (the Șuțu Palace). In former times, Bucharest was known as the "Little Paris". Today, the dynamic life of this fascinating metropolis, in step with the times, manifests a different kind of charm, which we invite you to discover for yourselves.

The Romanian Athenaeum (1886-1888), with its neoclassical facade and baroque cupola
Das Rumänische Athenäum (1886-1888) mit neoklassischer Fassade und einer Barockkuppel

The Hill of the Metropolis, on which are sited the Church of the Patriarchate, founded in 1656-1658 by Prince Constantin Șerban Basarab, the bell tower, built by Constantin Brâncoveanu in 1698, and the Palace of the Patriarchate
Der Metropoliehügel, auf dem sich die Patriarchatskirche erhebt, 1656-1658 vom Herrscher Constantin Șerban Basarab gestiftet, ferner der 1698 von Constantin Brâncoveanu erbaute Glockenturm sowie der Patriarchatspalast

Stadtansichten

Das Zusammentreffen von Neu und Alt, das uns in den rumänischen Städten begegnet, wirkt manchmal verwirrend. Die Bauten aus Beton und Glas, die Straßen voller betäubendem Gesumme, daneben Plätze, an denen bemerkenswerte Gebäude stehen, die von verschiedenen Stilarten geprägt sind, und einsame Straßen, in denen Kastanienbäume Schatten spenden. Hie und da trifft man auf Spuren des kommunistischen Regimes, unter dessen unheilvollem Zeichen Rumänien fast ein halbes Jahrhundert lang gestanden hat. Tausende alter Häuser wurden damals in den rumänischen Städten abgetragen, um Platz zu schaffen für unästhetische Einheitsbauten (Wohnblocks). Nach der Revolution von 1989, die zum Fall des Diktators Nicolae Ceaușescu und zur demokratischen Wende führte, haben sich in Rumänien die Gesetze der Marktwirtschaft durchgesetzt. Seither ist fast überall das Baufieber ausgebrochen, was eine spektakuläre und rapide Veränderung im Aussehen der großen Städte zur Folge hatte.

Bukarest, die Hauptstadt Rumäniens, ist eine europäische Stadt, die sich durch ihre glanzvollen Bauten auszeichnet: die Spar- und Depositenkasse, das Nationalmuseum für Geschichte, das Militärkasino, das Nationalmuseum für Kunst (der ehemalige Königspalast), die Zentrale Universitätsbibliothek (das einstige Palais der Universitätsstiftung Carol I.), das Rumänische Athenäum, das Museum George Enescu (im Palais Cantacuzino), das Museum für Geschichte des Munizipiums Bukarest (im Palais Șuțu). Einst wurde das elegante Bukarest „Klein-Paris" genannt. Nun strahlt das dynamische Leben dieser faszinierenden Metropole den heutigen Zeiten entsprechend einen andersartigen Zauber aus, wir laden Sie ein, diesen selbst zu entdecken.

The fountain at the centre of Luigi Cazzavillan Park, near Casa Radio
Der monumentale Brunnen im Park Luigi Cazzavillan in der Nähe des Rundfunkhauses

The Linden Inn: a shopping arcade built in 1833 and situated between Lipscani and Blănari streets in the historic centre of Bucharest
Hanul cu Tei (die Lindenherberge), ein aus kleinen Läden bestehender Geschäftskomplex, 1833 zwischen der Lipscani- und der Blănari-Straße im historischen Zentrum von Bukarest erbaut

The Macca-Villacrosse Passage,
opened in 1891, links Calea Victoriei
and Eugeniu Carada Street.
*Die Passage Macca-Villacrosse, 1891
eröffnet, verbindet die Calea Victoriei
mit der Eugeniu-Carada-Straße.*

The National Savings Bank Palace, built between
1896 and 1900 according to the plans of French
architect Paul Gottereau
*Der Palast der Spar- und Depositenbank (CEC) ist
1896-1900 nach den Plänen des französischen
Architekten Paul Gottereau erbaut worden*

The banks of the Dâmbovița River and University Square
Dâmbovița-Kai und Universitätsplatz, Nachtansichten

The twelfth century Saxon colonists in Transylvania developed a typically Germanic structure in this area. Sighişoara, the only inhabited mediaeval citadel in Southeast Europe, was declared a World Heritage Site by UNESCO in 1999. Sibiu, a modern, western city, still preserves traces of the flourishing mediaeval burg of former times, as well as buildings specific to the Viennese Baroque, built during the time of the Hapsburg Empire. Cluj-Napoca is one of Romania's major centres of culture and learning. There are nine institutes of higher learning here, with forty-nine faculties, and numerous research institutions.

The old centre of Baia Mare, situated at the foot of the Gutâi Mountains, is dominated by Stephen's Tower, surrounded by numerous recently restored baroque edifices. Visitors to Satu Mare are ravished by the architectural diversity of the city, where they can admire the baroque Reformed Church, the neo-classical Roman Catholic cathedral, the baroque and neo-Gothic Vácsay House, and the Secession White House.

Braşov, sited at the foot of the Tâmpa Mountain, is one of the most celebrated tourist centres in the country. Near the city can be found numerous remains of Saxon fortifications. In the city of Alba Iulia, the Act of Union between Romania and the provinces of Transylvania, Banat, Maramureş and Crişana was signed on 1 December 1918.

The Banat is synonymous with Timişoara, the city on the Bega River. Timişoara bears the most visible imprint of the Baroque: the old City Hall, the Palace of the Prefecture, the Roman Catholic Episcopal Palace, the St Catherine Roman Catholic Church etc. In Arad, you can visit a citadel dating from the sixteenth century, the Red Church, the Orthodox Cathedral, the Roman Catholic Church, the Serbian Church and the Palace of Culture.

The cities of Moldavia are bathed in a milder, more serene atmosphere. Here, time seems to move more slowly. This harmony is perhaps due to the dozens of monasteries founded in the immediate vicinity of the cities. In Moldavia, you will find settlements large (cities such as Suceava, Bacău, Galaţi, Piatra-Neamţ) and small (market towns like Vaslui, Focşani, Târgu Neamţ). The ineffably charming city of Iaşi, which, like Rome, is sited on seven hills, is without doubt the heart of Moldavia.

Romania's numerous spas (Băile Herculane, Sovata, Băile Felix, Slănic Moldova, Băile Olăneşti, Călimăneşti-Căciulata, Borsec, Tuşnad) and mountain resorts (Poiana Braşov, Sinaia, Buşteni, Predeal, Durău, Semenic, Muntele Mic) recommend it as an ideal place to spend your holidays.

Dobrogea is one of the most picturesque of the Romanian regions: the Black Sea coast, with the resorts of Mamaia, Eforie, Neptun, Costineşti, Saturn, Venus and Jupiter is invaded by thousands of tourists in the summer. In Constanţa (the ancient Greek colony of Tomis), a Black Sea port, the Genoese built a lighthouse in the thirteenth century, which is preserved to the present day. Over the settlements of Dobrogea still hovers the perfume of the Levant, reminding us of the times when the region was part of the Ottoman Empire (1417-1878).

The cities of Romania, large or small, old or new, constantly show that every place has its own way of surprising the traveller.

Peleş Castle at Sinaia, the former residence of the kings of Romania
Schloss Peleş in Sinaia, ehemalige Sommerresidenz der Könige Rumäniens

Die Siebenbürger Sachsen, die im 12. Jahrhundert in Transsilvanien angesiedelt wurden, haben in diesem Raum Niederlassungen gegründet, die eine typisch deutsche Struktur aufwiesen. Schäßburg (Sighişoara), die einzige bewohnte Burg Südosteuropas, wurde 1999 seitens der UNESCO zu einem Weltkulturerbe erklärt. Hermannstadt (Sibiu), eine moderne, westliche Stadt, bewahrt heute noch Spuren der einstigen blühenden mittelalterlichen Stadt und umfasst Bauten mit Architekturelementen, die für den Wiener Barock spezifisch sind und zur Zeit der habsburgischen Verwaltung entstanden. Klausenburg (Cluj-Napoca) ist ein bedeutendes kulturell-wissenschaftliches und Unterrichtszentrum Rumäniens. Hier gibt es 9 Hochschulen mit 49 Fakultäten und zahlreiche Forschungsinstitute. Das alte Zentrum von Baia Mare, der Stadt am Fuße der Gutâi-Berge, wird vom Stefansturm beherrscht. Rundum erheben sich zahlreiche, kürzlich renovierte Barockbauten. Wer Sathmar (Satu Mare) besucht hat, bleibt von der architektonischen Vielfalt der Stadt beeindruckt. Hier kann man u.a. die reformierte Kirche (die Kirche mit Ketten) im Barockstil, die römisch-katholische Kathedrale und das Bischofspalais in neuklassischem Stil, das Vácsay-Haus im Barock- und neugotischen Stil, das Weiße Haus im Sezessionsstil bewundern. Kronstadt (Braşov), am Fuße der Zinne (Tâmpa) gelegen, ist eines der größten Touristikzentren des Landes. In seiner Umgebung haben sich die Überreste zahlreicher sächsischer Befestigungen erhalten. In Alba Iulia ist am 1.Dezember 1918 der Akt der Vereinigung Transsilvaniens, des Banats, der Maramureş und des Kreischlandes mit Rumänien unterzeichnet worden.

Banat heißt Temeswar (Timişoara), die Stadt an der Bega, die Stadt, die hauptsächlich von Barockbauten geprägt ist (das alte Rathaus, das Palais der Präfektur, das römisch-katholische Bischofspalais, die römisch-katholische Kirche zur heiligen Katharina u.a.). In Arad können Sie eine Festung aus dem 16. Jahrhundert besichtigen, ferner die Rote Kirche, die orthodoxe Kathedrale, die römisch-katholische Kirche, die serbische Kirche, das Kulturpalais.

Die moldauischen Städte sind in eine sanftere, heitere Atmosphäre gehüllt. Hier scheint die Zeit noch Geduld zu haben. Diese Harmonie ist wohl auch den vielen Klöstern in nächster Nähe der Städte zu verdanken. Sie werden in der Moldau sowohl größere Städte antreffen (Suceava, Bacău, Galaţi, Piatra-Neamţ) als auch kleinere, die eher wie Marktflecken aussehen (Vaslui, Focşani, Târgu-Neamţ). Jassy (Iaşi), die Stadt auf sieben Hügeln wie Rom, ist selbstverständlich das Herz der Moldau. Ein Spaziergang durch Jassy gereicht unweigerlich zu einem großen Vergnügen.

Unzählige Bade- und Luftkurorte (Herkulesbad, Sovata, Felixbad, Slănic Moldova, Olăneşti, Călimăneşti-Căciulata, Borsec, Tuşnad) und Gebirgskurorte (Schulerau-Poiana Braşov, Sinaia, Buşteni, Predeal, Durău, Semenic, Muntele Mic) sind Grund genug, Rumänien als idealen Ferienort zu empfehlen.

Die Dobrudscha ist eine der malerischsten Gegenden Rumäniens: die Schwarzmeerküste mit den Seebädern Mamaia, Eforie, Neptun, Costineşti, Saturn, Venus, Jupiter ist im Sommer von Tausenden Touristen überlaufen. In Constanţa (der antiken griechischen Kolonie Tomis), der Hafenstadt am Schwarzen Meer, haben die Genueser im 13. Jahrhundert einen Leuchtturm gebaut, der heute noch steht. Über den Ortschaften der Dobrudscha schwebt noch immer ein levantinisches Aroma, das uns an die Zeiten erinnert, da dieses Gebiet von den Türken beherrscht wurde (1417-1878).

Die rumänischen Städte, größere oder kleinere, ältere oder neuere, beweisen uns immer wieder das Gleiche: Jeder Ort überrascht den Reisenden in seiner Art.

The Church of the Dormition of the Mother of God, in Council Square in Braşov
Die Kirche Mariä Himmelfahrt (Adormirea Maicii Domnului) am Rathausplatz in Kronstadt (Braşov)

The Central Markets in Ploieşti, designed by architect Toma T. Socolescu and built at the beginning of the twentieth century

Die Zentralen Markthallen in Ploieşti, Anfang des XX. Jahrhunderts nach den Plänen des Architekten Toma T. Socolescu erbaut

The ruins of the princely court at Târgovişte (the former capital of Wallachia), constructed successively by Mircea the Old, Petru Cercel, Matei Basarab, Radu the Great, and Constantin Brâncoveanu

Die Ruinen des Fürstenhofes in Târgovişte (ehemaliger Herrschersitz der Walachei). An diesem haben der Reihe nach die Fürsten Mircea der Alte (cel Batrân), Petru Cercel, Matei Basarab, Radu der Große (cel Mare) und Constantin Brâncoveanu bauen lassen

The Secession-style Palace of the Prefecture and the Palace of Culture in Târgu Mureş
Der Palast der Präfektur und das Kulturpalais im Sezessionsstil in Târgu Mureş

Sibiu, a mediaeval burg first attested in 1191, has been designated by the Council of Europe
as "European Capital of Culture" in 2007.
Hermannstadt (Sibiu), 1191 erstmals urkundlich erwähnt, wurde vom Europarat zur Europäischen Kulturhauptstadt des
Jahres 2007 gekürt.

The historic centre of Alba
Iulia is dominated by two
imposing edifices: the
Orthodox Cathedral of the
Holy Trinity and the Roman
Catholic Cathedral of
Saint Michael.
*Das Zentrum der Stadt
Alba Iulia wird von zwei
beeindruckenden Bauten
beherrscht: der orthodoxen
Kathedrale zur Heiligen
Dreieinigkeit und der
römisch-katholischen Kirche
zum Heiligen Michael.*

Sighişoara, the only
inhabited citadel in
south-east Europe, has
been designated a World
Heritage Site by UNESCO.
*Schässburg (Sighişoara),
die einzige bewohnte Burg
Südosteuropas, wurde ins
UNESCO-Weltkulturerbe
aufgenommen.*

The Hotel Dacia in Satu Mare, The Tower of Stephen in Baia Mare and the Roman Catholic Cathedral of Saint Michael in Cluj-Napoca
Das Hotel Dacia in Sathmar, der Stefansturm in Baia Mare und die römisch-katholische Kathedrale zum Heiligen Michael in Klausenburg (Cluj-Napoca)

The Orthodox cathedral of the Three Holy Hierarchs in Timişoara, The Palace of Culture in Arad
and The Black Eagle Passage in Oradea
Die orthodoxe Kathedrale der hl. Drei Hierarchen (Sfinţii Trei Ierarhi) in Temeswar (Timişoara),
Das Kulturpalais in Arad und die Einkaufspassage Schwarzer Adler (Vulturul Negru) in Oradea

The Museum of Argeş county in Piteşti, the statue representing Decebal in
Drobeta-Turnu Severin and Museum of Art in Craiova
*Das Kreismuseum aus Piteşti, die Statue Dezebals aus Drobeta-Turnu Severin
und das Kunstmuseum in Craiova*

The neo-Gothic edifice of the Palace of Culture (1907-1926) in Jassy (Iaşi), built on the site of the former courts, today houses an extensive museum complex.
Der neugotische Bau des Kulturpalastes von Jassy (Iaşi) (1907-1926) erhebt sich da, wo einst der Fürstenhof stand, und beherbergt heute einen großen musealen Komplex.

After Suceava became capital of Moldavia, in 1388, Prince Petru I Muşat built a citadel in the south-east quarter of the city, which was later extended by Stephen the Great.
Nachdem Suceava 1388 Hauptstadt der Moldau geworden war, baute der Fürst Petru I. Muşat im Südosten der Stadt eine Burg, die Stefan der Große später noch weiter ausbaute.

Tulcea – gateway to the Danube Delta
Tulcea – das „Eingangstor zum Donaudelta"

Aerial view over the shoreline of the maritime port of Constanța, dominated by the elegant silhouette of the Art Nouveau style Casino, built between 1907 and 1910
Luftbild von der Küstenpromenade des Touristenhafens von Constanța, die von der eleganten Silhouette des 1907-1910 im Jugendstil erbauten Kasinos beherrscht wird

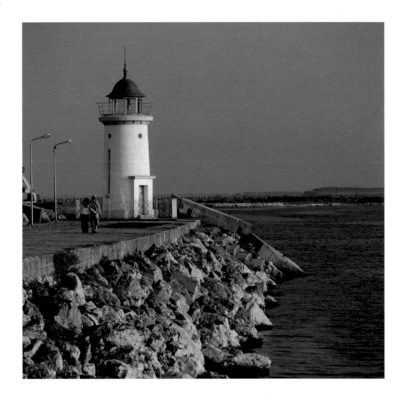

Our journey through Romania ends here… Behind us we leave beautiful moments, which will transform into memories, illumining our thoughts like the glimmer of a lighthouse.

Hier beenden wir unsere Reise durch Rumänien… Diese wunderschönen Augenblicke werden zurückbleiben, sich in Erinnerungen verwandeln und unsere Gedanken erhellen wie das funkelnde Aufleuchten eines Leuchtturms des Nachts.